CAJUN
Folktales

CAJUN
Folktales

By CELIA SOPER

Illustrated by PATRICK SOPER

PELICAN PUBLISHING COMPANY
Gretna 1997

*This book is dedicated to the memory of my father, Dr. Eric Guilbeau,
who first introduced me to Bouki and Lapin.*

Library of Congress Cataloging-in-Publication Data

Soper, Celia.
    Cajun folktales / Celia Soper ; illustrated by Patrick Soper.
      p. cm.
    Summary: Presents six folktales from southern Louisiana, featuring
Lapin the rabbit and Bouki, a coyote or wolf, and some of their
animal friends.
    ISBN 1-56554-257-6 (alk. paper)
    1. Tales—Louisiana. 2. Cajuns—Folklore. [1. Cajuns—Folklore.
2. Folklore—Louisiana.] I. Soper, Patrick, ill. II. Title.
PZ8.1.S667Caj 1997
398.2'09763'0452—dc21
[E]   97-16928
                                                  CIP
                                                  AC

Printed in Hong Kong

Published by Pelican Publishing Company, Inc.
1101 Monroe Street, Gretna, Louisiana 70053

CAJUN
Folktales

Introduction

Deep in south Louisiana lies Cajun country. Here two groups of French settlers, Creole blancs and Cajuns, made their homes in the eighteenth century.

These early settlers brought with them oral tales from their homeland. When they arrived they were introduced to a Negro population. These Creoles, descendants of African slaves, also had a rich oral tradition.

Their tales center mainly around Lapin, a rabbit, and Bouki, a coyote or wolf, his slow-witted *compère* or "friend."

The word *lapin* is French for "rabbit," but *bouki* is African for "hyena." Lapin became the symbol for cunning while Bouki represented the stupid or less quick-witted one.

Today the stories are being lost because the tradition of the oral tale is dying. Here are some of the best that are still alive in the memories of the Cajun people of south Louisiana.

The Farm

Bouki and Lapin had a farm that they worked together. One day in summer when the air was warm and smelled of honeysuckle, they strolled out to the field to see about the potato crop. It was a very good year and the potato plants were thick with leaves and full of pretty flowers. Bouki and Lapin stood a long time enjoying their handiwork.

"It will soon be time to dig our potatoes. How shall we divide our crop?" said Lapin. "Do you want to take the roots and I'll take the plants?"

"Oh, no!" exclaimed Bouki, looking at the lovely flowers. "I want the pretty plants."

They dug up the potato crop and Bouki took all the fine plants home to his storeroom. The flowers wilted, the leaves turned brown and fell off, the stalks became hard and dry. Bouki was left with nothing at all to eat!

Lapin took the roots home and stored them in his bins. It was a very large crop and Lapin dined royally all through the winter on potato soup, potato pancakes, potato stew, and french fries.

In the spring it was time to harvest the corn and once again Bouki and Lapin went out in the field together.

"Lapin will not get the best of me this time," thought Bouki. "I am ready for him and his tricks."

When Lapin said, "Well, Bouki, I give you first choice. Do you want the roots or the plants?"

"The roots, the roots," cried Bouki joyously. Quite excitedly, Bouki gathered all of the roots from the corn plants and took them home. He tried boiling them, he tried frying them, he even made a gumbo, but the roots remained hard and tough and dry!

Lapin had enough grain stored in his bins to have corn macque choux, corn bisque, corn on the cob, and grits and gravy all through the winter.

Bouki never could understand what happened to his crop, but he did decide one thing—never to farm with Compère Lapin again!

La Poussière

(The Dust)

Compère Chevreuil had a most beautiful daughter. She was easily the most-sought-after maid in the swamp. Compère Chevreuil decided to hold a grand ball at which he would give his daughter's hand in marriage to the suitor who could dance upon a rock until dust came out of it.

Soon the word spread throughout the great Atchafalaya Swamp and everyone began preparing for the grand event.

Compère 'Coon began fixing up early by bathing in Bayou Cocodrie, where the water was sweet and clear. Compère Fox shaved his moustache and brushed his fluffy tail until it shone. Compère Bouki, Compère Ours, and even Compère 'Possum, groomed until they were spic-and-span for the competition.

The only one who did not make any effort at all was Compère Lapin. He lay around in the dust all day and refused to get ready for the ball.

That night Compère Chevreuil brought a big, flat rock into the middle of the dance floor. All of the would-be suitors gathered around eagerly.

Compère Bouki tried first. He jumped and twirled about but could not raise even a little dust. Compère 'Coon came next and he danced his heart out, but to no avail. One after the other they tried—Compère Ours, Compère Alligator, even Compère Frog leapt and yelled and whooped—but no one made one speck of dust!

Only Lapin remained. He sat in the corner looking weak and tired. Compère Chevreuil took him by the hand and led him to the dance floor. Lapin approached the rock slowly, but as he mounted it, he began to jump and spin furiously. In a twinkling all the dust that he had gathered in his fur that afternoon began to fly about. It was so thick that the onlookers were blinded and everyone thought the dust had come from the rock. When Lapin finally quit dancing, and the dust settled, there he stood triumphantly!

That is how Lapin won the most beautiful bride in the swamp for his own.

Monsieur Tortie

A family lived on the banks of Bayou Vermilion. They hunted for food in the woods and swamps and fished in the stream for catfish, turtles, and garfish. One day the father, Monsieur LeBlanc, caught a large tortoise. He put it in a cage and went to invite his friends to take dinner with him, as turtle meat is a great delicacy. While he was gone, his little boy, André, went to the cage to see Monsieur Tortie. The tortoise began to whistle! André was delighted and asked him how he did it.

"Oh, that is nothing compared to what I will do if you will open the cage," said Monsieur Tortie. André did so and now Monsieur Tortie whistled the most beautiful melody while he danced around. André was enchanted with his magic turtle, who then said to him, "Put me on the banks of the bayou and you will see!"

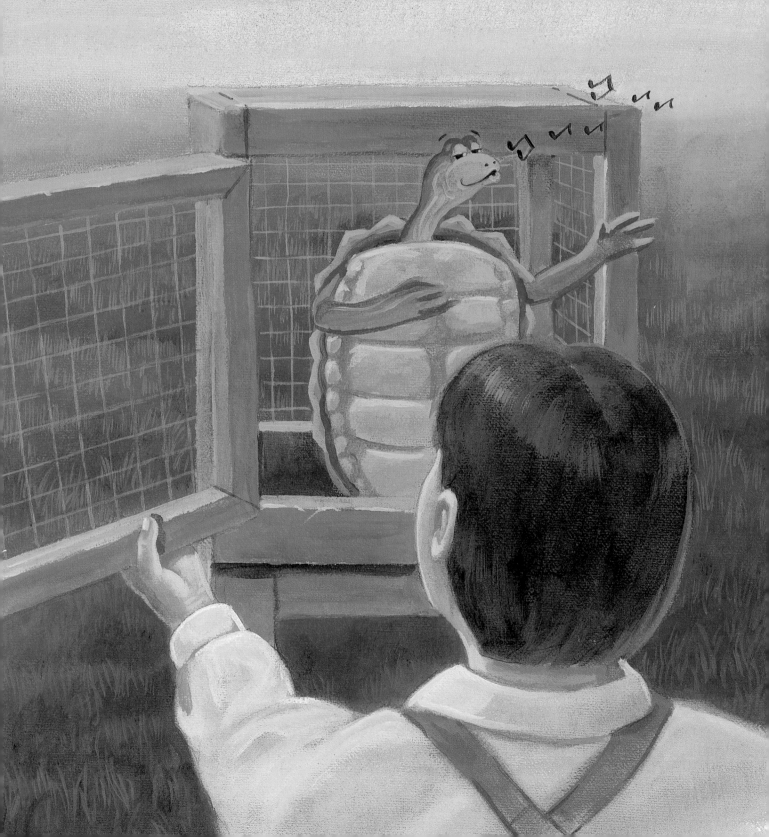

André could hardly wait, so he picked up the tortoise and ran to Bayou Vermilion. Monsieur Tortie sang and danced up a storm, then all of a sudden, he slipped off the bank and disappeared into the muddy water. André, kneeling on the bank, cried and called to Monsieur Tortie, but the tortoise only rose in the middle of the bayou and said, "Learn not to trust people whom you do not know!"

André was frightened that his father would punish him, so he put a large, flat stone into the cage. His mother, Clothile, didn't realize the turtle was now a stone. She put it into the roux to make a good turtle soup for her company. But she was astonished that the turtle remained hard for so long, so she called it to her husband's attention. Monsieur LeBlanc ordered the tortoise put on the table where he tried to cut it open with his carving knife. It was in vain. He took his hatchet, but to no avail. He took his axe to the tortoise, but he smashed the dishes, broke the table, and knocked over the chairs while the tortoise remained intact. He then finally took a closer look and saw it was a stone!

To this day Monsieur and Madame LeBlanc do not understand how Monsieur Tortie was turned to stone, and André has never told them!

Compère Lapin
and Madame Carencro

This is the story of Madame Carencro, a buzzard, and why all buzzards are bald.

Madame Carencro lived in the great Atchafalaya Swamp high up in an old cypress tree. Her husband was a lazy, old buzzard who never brought her and her babies enough to eat. In the base of the cypress tree was a big hole in which Compère Lapin lived. He was a good hunter and lived quite well off of all the wonderful food provided by the swamp. Each time Madame Carencro saw him, he seemed fatter and more tasty and she wished with all her might that she could eat him.

Well, one day it was just too much for Madame, so while Lapin was sleeping, she crept down the tree and closed up the hole with *bousillage* (mud and moss). Now Compère Lapin could not get out and would die of hunger!

When Lapin woke up he begged Madame Carencro to let him out but she only refused, saying, "I am hungry and need food." As soon as Compère Lapin realized he was caught for sure, he quit begging and did not make a sound.

Madame Carencro forgot caution and began to lick her lips as she thought about her wonderful rabbit sauce piquante. She put her ear to the hole and since she could hear nothing, she decided Lapin had smothered. But the only way to be sure was to remove the bousillage from the hole. As she did so, Lapin leapt past her and ran off shouting, "You see, it is you who are caught and not I!"

Compère Lapin went to his friend Bouki's house to live for a while since he was afraid to return to his tree. He was standing by the door a few days later when he spied Madame Carencro and her children out for a walk. The sight of her made Lapin so mad he ran to the kitchen and snatched up a large pan full of burning embers and hot ashes. As the family passed Bouki's home, Compère Lapin dashed out and threw the hot coals on them.

Buzzards have very thick feathers except on the top of their heads, so they shook the embers off quickly but not before their head feathers had burned down to the skin.

This is why all buzzards are bald to this day. And Compère Lapin? He has returned to his home in the cypress tree because from that day on, buzzards never eat rabbits!

Compère Crapaud's Ride

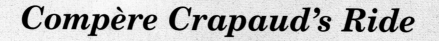

Compère Chevreuil and Compère Crapaud were both in love with the same girl. They were always fighting over her so finally they asked her to choose between them. She did not want to hurt anyone's feelings so she proposed a contest.

"You can have a race and the one who gets here first on Sunday is the one I shall marry," she told them.

Now Compère Chevreuil, being a deer, was certain he could beat Compère Crapaud, who was merely a toad. He agreed quite readily.

Strangely enough, Compère Crapaud seemed happy with the contest also and agreed to meet the deer at his home on Sunday before the race.

When they were ready, they took off like a shot with Compère Chevreuil in the lead. Just as the deer flashed by, the little toad caught onto his tail and stayed there. Taking in the fresh breeze the whole way, the toad throughly enjoyed himself.

Compère Chevreuil arrived at his beloved's house seemingly alone and she invited him in. Although she didn't want to hurt Compère Crapaud's feelings, she was happy that the deer had won because he was more elegant and handsome than the squatty, green toad.

"Have a chair," she said, but when Compère Chevreuil went to sit down, Compère Crapaud jumped on the chair and cried, "Wait awhile, you are sitting on me! I was here first."

Compère Chevreuil could plainly see that Compère Crapaud had beat him to the house, so he had no recourse but to admit defeat.

That is how Compère Crapaud won himself a beautiful bride, proving that careful plans can turn the tide even when the outcome seems certain.

The Escape

Because Compère Lapin was smaller than most of the creatures in the swamp, he had to be more cunning. He always had to use either his swiftness or his brains to avoid disaster.

One day Lapin was rolling around in the fragrant grass along the bayou banks. He had eaten so much he could hardly move, when who should suddenly loom into view but Compère Ours!

Now Lapin was fast on his feet but today he was so full he could barely move and Compère Ours was lumbering closer by the minute!

Compère Lapin rolled over, stuck his feet straight up in the air, and played dead!

A bear may be very big and powerful, but Lapin was by far the more cunning of the two. When Compère Ours lumbered up on Lapin, he just shook his head and said, "Too bad that rabbit's so small or I would certainly eat him for dinner. But just one would be too much trouble to fool with." He walked on down Bayou LaFourche looking for crawfish to add to his meal.

Now Lapin couldn't resist playing with Compère Ours. He circled wide around him and lay down "dead" in his path once more.

When Ours came up upon this scene again, he stopped and scratched his head. It occurred to him that he could profit by this apparent "rabbit kill," so he said, "What a shame! And this one's as fat as the last one. I could make a really fine rabbit sauce piquante!"

Lapin just stayed as still as he could. All Compère Ours had to do was reach down with his huge powerful paws and he would be done for!

Just as Ours was bending down, he had a bright idea. "I think I'll go back and pick up that first rabbit and then return for this one," he exclaimed, and so he ambled off.

Poor Ours, he didn't have rabbit sauce piquante for supper. Lapin was miles down the road in two shakes of a lamb's tail. Compère Ours had to settle for crawfish étouffée!

Glossary

Term	Pronunciation	Definition
Atchafalaya	a-chaf-a-LEYE-a	a swamp in Louisiana
bouki	boo-KEE	hyena or wolf
bousillage	boo-see-AHJ	mud and moss
chevreuil	shuh-VRol	deer
carencro	cair-en-CROH	buzzard
cocodrie	co-co-DREE	crocodile or alligator
Compère	cohm-PAIR	friend
'coon	coon	raccoon
crapaud	cra-POH	toad
étouffée	ay-too-FAY	smothered dish
gumbo	GUM-boh	a kind of soup
lapin	lah-PAN	rabbit
madame	ma-DAHM	Mrs.
monsieur	muh-SYUR	Mr.
ours	ors	bear
'possum	POSS-uhm	opossum
poussière	poo-see-AIR	dust
sauce piquante	sauce pee-KAHNT	flavorful stew
tortie or *tortue*	tor-TEE or tor-TOO	turtle